FACT or PHONY?

YOU CAN GET SUCKED DOWN AN AIRPLANE TOILET!

The Fact or Fiction Behind URBAN MYTHS

PAUL MAS

Gareth St
PUBLISHING

Please visit our website, **www.garethstevens.com**.
For a free color catalog of all our high-quality books,
call toll free 1-800-542-2595 or fax 1-877-542-2596.

Cataloging-in-Publication Data

Mason, Paul.
The fact or fiction behind urban myths / by Paul Mason.
p. cm. — (Fact or phony?)
Includes index.
ISBN 978-1-4824-4274-8 (library binding)
1. Common fallacies — Juvenile literature.
I. Mason, Paul, 1967-. II. Title.
AZ999.M37 2016
001.9'6—d23

Published in 2016 by
Gareth Stevens Publishing
111 East 14th Street, Suite 349
New York, NY 10003

Editor: Debbie Foy
Design: Rocket Design (East Anglia) Ltd
Illustration: Alan Irvine

All illustrations by Shutterstock, except 4, 9, 15, 16, 25, 27, 40, 60, 63 and 84.

Printed in the United States of America
CPSIA compliance information: Batch CW16GS: For further information contact Gareth Stevens, New York, New York at 1-800-542-2595.

read on!

If you've ever heard the expression "old wives' tale," you'll already have a pretty good idea of what constitutes an urban myth. They're facts or advice that we've all heard, without knowing whether they're exactly true or not. "A dog's bite is cleaner than a human's" is one example.

"At least it'll be a clean bite. Won't it?"

The Internet has given many urban myths and legends a new lease of life. Things people would never believe if they were just told them take on the ring of truth once they appear on screen.

The Internet has also been responsible for the spread of another kind of urban myth: the incredible-but-apparently-true-story...

These were often first cut and pasted from news articles — usually joke ones that people haven't realized are jokes. The next thing you know, the story is popping into your inbox, with a heading saying something like:

READ THIS! — urgent information about [add amazing topic here]. IT COULD SAVE LIVES!

FACT OR PHONY takes a long hard look at some of the most popular urban myths. Is it true, for example, that Friday the 13th is an unlucky day? Or that people whose eyes are close together are untrustworthy? That America's missions to the Moon never really happened, or that space is full of junk left by astronauts? There are people who will swear these things are fact — so, with a copy of this book in your hand, you'll be ready to tell them whether or not they're correct!

Of course, it's not only the facts behind urban myths that people regularly get wrong. So we also investigate some of the other "facts" that people have been mistaken about over the years. Whoever thought a machine for massaging your eyeballs was a good idea, for example? Or that Swiss roll cakes actually came from Switzerland? Or that TV would never become popular?

"There's one born every minute," they say, to describe suckers who'll believe nearly anything. Armed with a copy of this book, at least that sucker won't be you!

read on!

So you might hear myths like...

> ### Wait 30 minutes after eating before swimming, or you'll drown

This myth is a favorite with grandmothers and great aunts, and is a variation on, "Let your food go down before you play football, go outside, strap on your Rollerblades or even *think* about having any kind of fun."

It's based on the idea that after you've eaten, your stomach needs oxygen to help it digest your food. But, of course, your muscles also need oxygen, and so if you go for a swim while your stomach's busy digesting food, the oxygen won't be available to your muscles. According to the myth, you'll be too weak to keep swimming and will, most likely, drown.

★ And the truth is...

In fact, your body takes in more than enough oxygen for movement *and* digestion. And as if that wasn't enough, your digestive system automatically shuts down within a minute or so after you start exercising.

Verdict:  **PHONY**

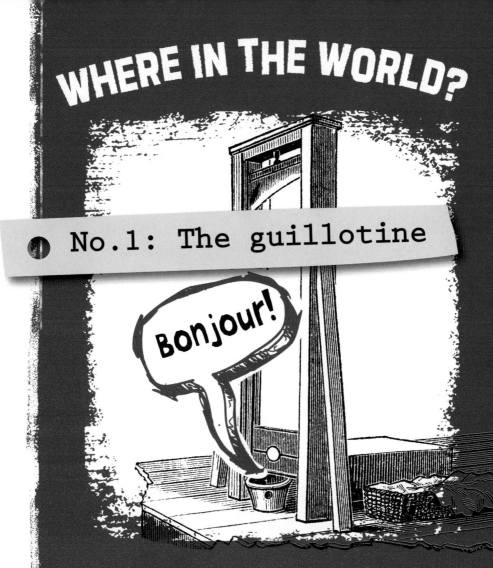

No.1: The guillotine

Bonjour!

The guillotine sounds French, right? French revolutionaries certainly made this device famous when they started using it for chopping off people's heads in the 1790s. All in all, they managed to part at least 15,000 citizens from their *têtes*.

But despite being named after a Frenchman, Dr. Guillotine, the chopping device was actually invented in Halifax, Yorkshire, in the UK. There, the "Halifax Gibbet" was first used to execute criminals in 1286.

IT'LL NEVER WORK!

"Heavier-than-air flying machines are impossible"

Lord Kelvin (1824-1907),
British scientist
and mathematician

If you swallow an orange seed, an orange tree will grow inside you

One popular way for parents to frighten their children is to tell them that swallowing fruit seeds will cause a tree to grow inside their stomachs. Some even go so far as to say that the branches will eventually come out of their ears or mouth!

As well as scaring children, this myth puts them off eating fruit — which parents are always trying to get their kids to do. Which just goes to show how dumb some adults are.

The theory goes that plants need a) warmth and b) fluid. Since your insides are warm and full of fluid, the seed will germinate and grow into a plant.

⭐ And the truth is...

Maybe this myth grew from the knowledge that some seeds are poisonous, so it's a bad idea to eat them.* But plants need light to grow — and if there's any light getting into your insides, there's *definitely* something wrong. Also, the juices in your stomach are acidic, and would kill a plant even if one *could* start growing.

Verdict:  PHONY

*See pages 16 and 17.

YOU ONLY USE 10% OF YOUR BRAIN

There are several different versions of this myth:

1

You only use 10% of your brain

Apparently, researchers have hooked people up to machines that provide an image of what their brain is doing. The bits where there's something going on light up in color. Amazingly, when they ask people to think about something or perform an action, it's clear that only 10% of the brain is being used!

TEN PERCENT? AS MUCH AS THAT?

10

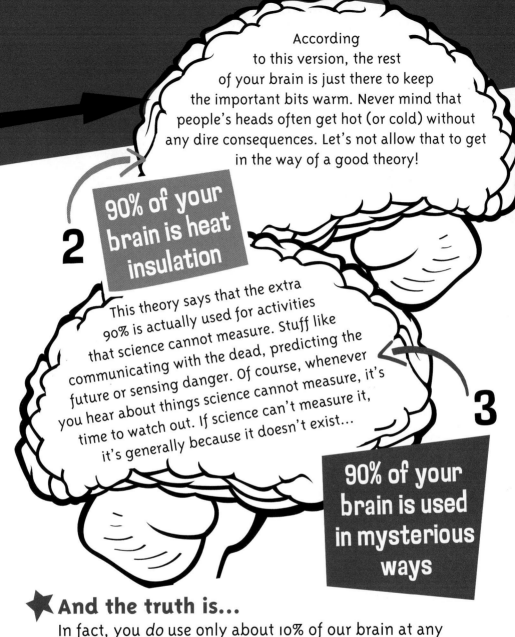

According to this version, the rest of your brain is just there to keep the important bits warm. Never mind that people's heads often get hot (or cold) without any dire consequences. Let's not allow that to get in the way of a good theory!

2 90% of your brain is heat insulation

This theory says that the extra 90% is actually used for activities that science cannot measure. Stuff like communicating with the dead, predicting the future or sensing danger. Of course, whenever you hear about things science cannot measure, it's time to watch out. If science can't measure it, it's generally because it doesn't exist...

3 90% of your brain is used in mysterious ways

★ And the truth is...

In fact, you *do* use only about 10% of our brain at any one time — but that's not the same as saying the other 90% is never used. We use different bits of our brains for different things, and not all of them are used at the same time.

Verdict: a bit true — but mainly 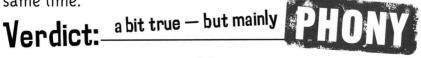 PHONY

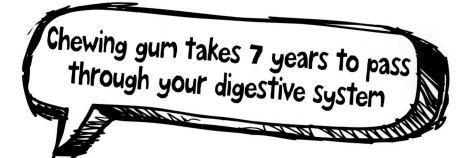

Chewing gum takes 7 years to pass through your digestive system

Most of us have been told this by our parents at some time or another. Another version of the saying goes that the sticky gum will wrap itself around your internal organs and may even clog up your insides!

The thinking behind the chewing gum warnings goes like this:

> *Chewing gum isn't food — and you shouldn't swallow things that aren't food, right?*

> *Chewing gum's sticky: once it's inside you, it will just stick to your insides and take ages to come out.*

★ And the truth is...

Chewing gum isn't especially sticky after you've swallowed it, and there's no special reason why it should a) take a long time to pass through your digestive system or b) get wrapped around your organs.

People have had the chewing habit for hundreds of years — in fact since long before chewing gum was even invented. (Before gum, people used to chew tree resin.) Humans have *always* chewed resin or gum, and they've probably *always* swallowed it from time to time.

Verdict:  PHONY

You can cook an egg with two mobile phones

The instructions for anyone wanting to do this (no one ever explains *why* you'd want to cook an egg using mobile phones) are as follows:

1. **Place an uncooked egg between two mobile phones, with the phones facing each other.**

2. **Call one phone from the other. Nothing will happen for the first 15 minutes (except for your call charges racking up). After that, the egg starts to cook.**

3. **After 65 minutes, end the call, then break the egg open. You will find that it's cooked.**

★ And the truth is...

When mobile phones first appeared on the scene, there were all kinds of scare stories about them. Some people even claimed they would fry your brain. This particular story was cooked up (ha!) in 2000 as a spoof.

Verdict:  PHONY

A bolt of lightning cannot harm you in a vehicle with rubber tires

Many people will tell you that the safest place to be during a thunderstorm is in a car, van, or truck with rubber tires.

This idea is based on the fact that rubber is an insulator against electricity. Since electricity cannot pass through rubber, sitting in a car with rubber tires means electricity will not be able to pass through it or you. Some people even say that wearing rubber boots, or riding a bicycle with rubber tires, will keep you from being fried by lightning.

And the truth is...

A car IS a relatively safe place to be during a thunderstorm — but it has nothing to do with the tires, which cannot resist the electrical charge of a lightning strike. In fact, the metal shell of the car acts as a safety cage. The electricity runs around the outside of the car — but so as long as you're not touching metal, it won't affect you.

Verdict: a teeny bit true — but mainly **PHONY**

IT'LL NEVER HAPPEN!

"They couldn't hit an elephant at this dist..."

The final words of General John Sedgwick, to an underling trying to warn him of danger during the Battle of Spotsylvania in 1864.

Eating apple seeds can poison you!

We all know stories about people (usually princesses) being poisoned or sent to sleep by apples. But they're just fairy tales, right? Even so, people will still insist to you that you really mustn't eat apple seeds, because they contain poison.

Yes, it's the seeds that can hurt you!

16

You might even hear someone saying that cherry pits, or the pits of peaches and apricots, are poisonous too. Of course, this must be nonsense: things millions of people eat every day can't be poisonous. Can they?

 ## And the truth is...

Apple seeds contain a substance called amygdalin. When this is digested, it turns into hydrogen cyanide. (Hydrogen cyanide is the deadly chemical the Nazis used to kill people in concentration camps during World War II.)

The good news is that apple seeds have a hard outer shell, which means they normally pass through your insides without being digested. Plus, you'd have to eat literally TONS of apples to be poisoned.

Cherry pits, as well as peach and apricot pits, also contain amygdalin. Of course, these come with a rock-hard protective outer layer, which would be rather uncomfortable to swallow. But the pits of peaches and apricots do contain enough amygdalin to be harmful.

Verdict: mostly FACT

> ## On average, women swallow 4.4 to 9 pounds (2-4 kg) of lipstick during their lifetime

When women put on lipstick, many of them rub their lips together. The story goes that a little bit of it always ends up in their mouth, and then gets swallowed. More lipstick can get swallowed while licking lips, eating, and drinking. Incredibly, during a woman's lifetime, she will end up swallowing at least 4.4 pounds (2 kg) of the stuff!

This myth has been reported in newspapers and magazines all round the world, from Australia to the UK, Canada, and the USA.

★ And the truth is...

A stick of lipstick weighs 2-3 grams, less than $\frac{1}{10}$ of an ounce. So even the lowest estimate — 4.4 pounds (2 kg) — would be 667 whole sticks of lipstick. To reach 9 pounds (4 kg), a woman would have to swallow 1,334 entire sticks. Both these figures seem unlikely.

Say you get 200 applications from a stick: 667 sticks equals about 133,400 applications. A woman who starts wearing lipstick at 15 and stops at 65 has 18,262.5 possible days of lipstick-wearing in between. She'd have to be putting on a fresh coat of lipstick 7 or 8 times a day, every day, even to USE 9 pounds (2 kg) of lipstick — let alone swallow it.

Verdict:  PHONY

WHERE IN THE WORLD?

Most people think that poodles come from France, but they're actually German. Their name comes from the German word "pudelhund."

Poodles were bred partly for swimming, and some people claim that their strange pom-pom haircuts were intended to keep their joints warm while in the water.

> ## A special chemical in swimming pools turns red if you pee in the water

Imagine this: you're swimming along happily, and suddenly people swimming around you start to scream and head for the edges of the pool. A cloud of red appears around you in the water. Has a shark somehow gotten into the pool and bitten you? Of course not! You've done a naughty pee, and Urine Alert Dye™ has made the water go red.

Adults like to warn young people at every opportunity about the special chemical in swimming pools that turns red (or sometimes green or blue) if someone does a pee in the water. The idea is so popular that it's even made it into the movies, in the 2010 film *Grown Ups*. But is the story true?

★ And the truth is...

Urine Alert Dye™ doesn't exist. In fact, it would probably be almost impossible to make. You'd need to find something in pee for the dye to react with. But any chemical in pee would probably also be in the pool from other sources, such as sweat, so the water would constantly be red. This is a story put out by lifeguards and parents to keep kids in line.

Verdict:  PHONY

Peeing on a live rail will electrocute you

Peeing in the pool is embarrassing (as well as being a revolting thing to do), but it won't actually *kill* you. But the saying goes that if you pee on a live train track, you won't have the luxury of being embarrassed — you'll be dead! Which would come as a nasty shock, even to someone dumb enough to go anywhere NEAR a live train line!

The idea is that, because electricity passes through water, the power of the rail will zip up the stream of pee and hit your body. You'll quickly be doing an impression of a dead person — except it won't be an impression.

★ And the truth is...

In theory this is possible, so DON'T TRY IT. But in practice, it would be very unlikely. Almost as soon as it starts to come out, the stream of pee begins to break up into drops, with air gaps between them. Electricity would not pass along this. So to be electrocuted you'd have to be crouching SO close to the rail that you'd be almost touching it — which would be pretty dumb.

Verdict: theoretically possible — but mainly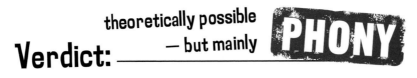

A tooth left in a glass of Coke will dissolve overnight

This is a favorite of grown-ups who are trying to explain why you don't need another soda. There are other versions, including the story of a piece of meat, left in a glass of Coke overnight, which had completely dissolved by the morning. It's also been claimed that there's something in Coke that will clean coins, and even eat away at marble steps!

★ And the truth is...

This myth started when a university professor told the US government that a tooth left in a glass of Coke would *begin* to soften and dissolve in 2 days. He blamed the sugar and phosphoric acid the drink contains. It's true that these can rot teeth, but it takes a long time. After you drink Coke, your saliva washes away most of the sugar and acid, preventing your teeth from rotting away. Anything remaining is brushed off when you brush your teeth (which you do twice a day, don't you?).

Verdict:

orange juice is bad for your teeth

This sounds crazy, right?

The idea that something as healthy as orange juice could rot your teeth is just ridiculous.

But then again...

 The truth is...

Remember the sugar and phosphoric acid in Coke on page 22? Well, there's a lot more of it in orange juice. In fact, there's almost twice as much of the acid in orange juice as in Coke.

This acid eats into the surface of your teeth, making them slightly softer than usual. Normally this isn't a big problem, because your teeth harden again in about an hour. But if you brush your teeth just after drinking orange juice (or other fruit juices), you're actually brushing away the protective layer. Eventually your teeth will rot away, and you'll look like a toothless character in a fairy tale. Yuck.

Verdict: mostly  **FACT**

Vampires do exist — and their hair and nails keep growing after they're buried

In the olden days, mysterious deaths or illnesses were sometimes blamed on vampires. People often decided to dig up the body of someone who had recently died, just to check they hadn't become a vampire.

Often, the corpse's fingernails and hair were longer than they had been when the person died. If they believed the corpse was a vampire, the body would have a stake driven through its heart (during which time the body would sometimes emit a long groan!), have garlic stuffed in its mouth, have its head cut off or be burned. Sometimes — on the basis that with vampires it's better to be safe than sorry — more than one of these things.

And the truth is...

When people die, fluids drain from their skin, which shrinks as a result. This can make the hair and nails (and sometimes even teeth) *seem* longer than they were before, but in fact it's just that they're more visible.

Dead bodies soon start to decompose, which causes gases to be released inside them. These gases may cause the body to make a noise (which could sound like a groan) when a stake is driven through its heart.

Verdict: PHONY

IT'LL NEVER HAPPEN!

"It will be years — not in my time — before a woman will become Prime Minister."

Margaret Thatcher speaking in 1969, ten years before becoming Prime Minister of the UK. As you can probably tell from the fact that her name was Margaret, Mrs. T was herself a woman!

Take our
HITLER QUIZ

Take our quiz to decide which of the following is true:

AFTER THE WAR, HITLER WENT ON A SOUTH AMERICAN HOLIDAY

Some people claim that Hitler was taken to Argentina in a "ghost convoy" of ships no one would admit to seeing, accompanied by two U-boats. He lived in South America for the rest of his life.

HITLER GETS CHILLY IN THE ANTARCTIC!

Other stories claim that Hitler went into hiding at a secret Nazi military base in the Antarctic. Again, he allegedly traveled there by U-boat. When the base was discovered in the 1950s, it was destroyed using atomic weapons.

HITLER ZOOMS TO THE MOON!

This theory — which can really only be described as crackpot — suggests that the Nazis reached the Moon in 1942 and set up a base. Hitler fled there, possibly with the help of UFOs, in 1944.

BURIED IN THE RUBBLE

Hitler shot himself with Russian troops banging on the steel door of his bunker, and his body was later taken back to Russia.

Answers:

So could any of numbers 1 to 3 be true?

Well, no:

1 Two U-boats did arrive in Argentina in 1945, at the end of the war — and then surrendered. They were not part of a "ghost convoy."

2 The German military did not visit Antarctica. U-boats could not have left passengers on land and the closest an atomic detonation got to Antarctica in the 1950s was 2,250 miles (3,620 km) away.

3 The Nazis did not visit the Moon. If they had, they would definitely not have found any air to breathe!

Only number 4 fits the facts.

Blonde people are slowly going to die out

The basis of this idea is that the gene determining hair color is weaker in blonde people (or red-haired people) than in dark-haired people. So if a blonde person and a dark-haired person have children, the children will have dark hair more often than not. The only way for blondes to survive is to have children only with other blondes. But ridiculously, given that their very survival is at stake, they keep getting together with *dark-haired people!*

★ And the truth is...

There's no actual evidence for any of this. The research is often said to have come from the World Health Organization, but they deny any knowledge of it. So this must be a story made up by someone who wishes they had blonde hair, but doesn't.

Verdict:  PHONY

⭐ Food-related inventions you probably haven't heard of before

Over the years, people have come up with some, um, "novel" inventions involving food.

Here are a couple of the tastiest examples:

1 The motorized ice cream cone

Described by the inventors as a "novelty amusement eating receptacle" for eating ice cream. The cone rotated, making this product especially useful for people who are simply too lazy to lick!

2 The pizza cone

This curiosity is like an ice cream cone (a normal one, not a motorized one), but made out of pizza crust! Fill it up with the kind of stuff that normally goes on a pizza and there you have it — a pizza cone! Er, yum…?

Friday the 13th is unlucky

Fear that bad things will happen on Friday the 13th is so common among some people that it has even been given a name: *paraskevidekatriaphobia*. (Some sources say that once you can pronounce this, you're cured.)

This myth grew out of two separate ideas: firstly, that Fridays are unlucky, and secondly that anything to do with the number 13 is also terribly unlucky!

1 Fridays are unlucky

The idea that Friday is an unlucky day has been around for hundreds of years, since at least the 1600s. Although generally a bad day to do *anything*, there were some activities people said you should never, ever begin on a Friday:

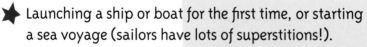 Launching a ship or boat for the first time, or starting a sea voyage (sailors have lots of superstitions!).

 Harvesting crops.

Getting married, giving birth (not that women have much choice about which day they do that), getting out of bed for the first time after being ill, or starting a new job.

2 Thirteen is an unlucky number

The idea that the number 13 is unlucky is sometimes said to come from ancient Norse myths. The legend goes that the goddess Frigga was banished to a mountaintop, where every Friday she would gather with 11 witches and the Devil — making 13 of them in total.

Other people claim that the source of the myth is numerology, the ancient study of the mystical significance of numbers. According to numerology, 12 was thought of as a "complete" number, because there were 12 months of the year, 12 signs of the zodiac, 12 hours on a clock, 12 apostles of Jesus, etc. Adding one to make 13 creates a bad number.

 And the truth is...

In any large group of people, there's bound to be someone who can tell you about someone else who had terrible things happen to them on Friday the 13th. Of course, terrible things also happen on Wednesday the 22nd, Sunday the 3rd, Thursday the 25th, etc, etc. But no one asks about that, or remembers it!

Verdict:  PHONY

It's possible to be sucked into an airplane toilet

"I heard of a woman on an Air France flight who pushed the flush button accidentally, and her bottom was sucked down into the toilet. She was so stuck that firemen had to free her when the flight landed."

This is a brilliant example of an urban myth, which usually happens to someone else. And airplane toilets certainly do flush very strongly, as anyone who's heard the *WHOOSH!* of air as they flush will agree.

⭐ And the truth is...

The suction created by an airplane toilet flushing is not strong enough to wedge a person into the bowl. Plus, all toilets have a little gap at the front and space between the seat and the top of the toilet bowl. This would make it impossible for anyone to get sealed onto the seat.

Verdict:  **PHONY**

You're taller in the morning than in the evening

Imagine you want to join the army. But there's a minimum height requirement: you have to be 5 ft, 8 in (173 cm) tall. You get a friend to measure you and — disaster — you're roughly an inch (2 cm) short! Then the friend says, hang on, we'll measure you again in the morning. Everyone knows we're all taller first thing in the morning: you'll be the right height then.

Could it work?

★ And the truth is...

All through the day, gravity acts on our bodies. It squishes down our knee joints and our spines, slowly forcing the bones closer together. Each joint is only affected a tiny bit, but they all add up. When we lie down to go to sleep again, the joints return to their natural position, a little bit further apart. So you are taller in the morning than the evening, by roughly 1 inch (2 cm).

Verdict:  FACT

Green cars are unlucky

It's said that people learning to drive will often refuse to take lessons in a green car, because they think it's an unlucky color and it will be impossible to pass their test. Racing drivers apparently hate competing in green cars, because it's impossible to win in one, and they're more likely to crash.

In fact, it's not only cars: green boats are said to be unlucky. It's also claimed to be very bad luck to wear green at a wedding. Actors also think that green is an unlucky color (mind you, actors have almost as many superstitions as sailors).

And the truth is...

This myth may have grown out of early racing accidents involving green cars. In 1911, 11 people were killed in Syracuse, New York, when a green race car crashed. Then in 1920, famous driver Gaston Chevrolet died after a green car hit his own. But no statistics show that green cars are more likely to crash, or are unlucky in any other way.

Though green is considered unlucky in the UK, US and Canada, in other places, such as Islamic countries, green is thought to be the color of paradise!

Verdict:

You should open a window during a tornado

After a destructive tornado, some houses are left looking as if they have been blown apart. The windows, doors and sometimes even the walls are blown outward, as if a bomb has gone off inside.

In areas where tornados strike, you often hear people say that it's a good idea to open windows slightly when twisters are forecasted. Apparently this will stop extreme air pressure from building up inside during the storm, making your house less likely to explode.

★ And the truth is...

In fact, your home is more likely to be blown apart if you open a window: the wind will get inside and lift off the roof, after which the walls may fall or be blown outward. This is what has happened to buildings that are blown apart during a tornado.

Verdict:  **PHONY**

⭐ Toilet inventions you probably haven't heard of before

There aren't many things worse than walking into the bathroom than finding that either a) the person in there before you wasn't a very good shot or b) they've left an unpleasant souvenir behind. Maybe that's where the ideas for these inventions came from?

1 Aim for the bull's-eye This invention is exactly what it says: a target pattern fixed to the back of the bowl, showing men where to, erm, aim.

2 Fire at the buzzer Another invention that aimed to give males something to shoot at, this device involved sensors on the toilet to detect pee. They would then trigger an LED lamp or buzzer. Whether a buzzer going off would have helped with the target practice is uncertain….

3 The poo scale This very old patent from 1924 allowed you to weigh your poo before flushing it away. This must have made trips to the toilet far more interesting and educational!

HICCUP QUIZ

There are hundreds of myths about hiccups and how to cure them: so many, there isn't space here to list them all. An Internet search for "cures for hiccups" will turn up some really loopy ones, such as "breathe through a wet washcloth" or other such foolish remedies.

Hiccups happen when your diaphragm (the stretchy barrier between the lungs and abdomen) suddenly tightens. Which of these cures do you think would work?

1. Drinking backward

Drinking a glass of water backward — from the part of the rim furthest from you — is claimed to cure hiccups. If you can stop yourself from laughing and spraying water all down your front, that is.

2. Standing on your head

The idea here is that with gravity pulling your insides in a new direction, everything will reset itself. Of course, gravity will be pulling your entire insides in the same direction, so it's not clear why this would work. But still — worth a try just for the fun of trying to stand on your head.

3. Mind control

There are lots of versions of this, but the basic idea is to distract yourself from your hiccups. You could:

- ★ Try to remember all the bald men you know.
- ★ Stare at something really, really hard.
- ★ Imagine a sign blinking on and off, faster and faster.

4. Scare the hiccups away

The idea here is to give someone such a fright that their stomach gives a little jump — curing their hiccups. Creeping up behind them, giving a sudden shout, pinching their arm, or even kissing them suddenly has been recommended!

Answers

Hiccups are mysterious — it is not completely understood why they happen. This means it's not possible to say whether or why any of the cures listed above work. But hiccups almost always go away within an hour. If you have hiccups for longer — overnight, say — see a doctor.

39

"At least it'll be a clean bite. Won't it?"

A dog's bite is cleaner than a human's

People will tell you that, if you have a choice between being bitten by a human or by a dog, you should pick the dog. (People who give you this advice always seem to forget that dogs are MUCH better at biting than humans — but let's leave that aside for now.) The dog's mouth is cleaner, they say, so there's less chance of the bite getting infected....

★ And the truth is...

You don't have to think about this for very long to realize it may not be true. Dogs use their mouths for everything, including picking up dead rats, licking their private parts, eating, and biting. Their mouths *can't* be as clean as someone who brushes their teeth and only uses their mouth for eating, talking and kissing! BUT, the things that make a bite likely to become infected are bacteria. Bacteria are mostly species-specific, so dog bacteria are harmful to dogs, human bacteria to humans. If a dog bites you, it delivers dog bacteria into the wound. This is less likely to be harmful. It doesn't mean a dog's bite is cleaner — just that it comes with the "right" kind of dirt.

Verdict: nearly ★ FACT

WHERE IN THE WORLD?

No.3:
Chicken tikka masala

Wowzer! This gravy packs a punch!

You would assume that the delicious curry dish chicken tikka masala was invented in India, right?

Wrong. In the 1970s, when a man in an Indian restaurant in the Scottish city of Glasgow asked for gravy with his meat, the chef didn't know what gravy was, and so mixed together tomato soup, spices, and yogurt. Chicken tikka masala was born.

Today, chicken tikka masala is often said to be the most popular meal in Britain. It even rivals fish and chips as the country's national dish.

You can tell someone's character from how they look

There are lots of myths about how you can tell what a person is like from their appearance. Just apply a few simple rules based on well-known guidelines and, hey presto! You'll know exactly what kind of person you're dealing with.

Here are just a few of the most popular myths:

"A weak chin shows lack of determination"

Chins are said to be a reliable way of forecasting someone's character. The "weak chin = lack of determination" myth is very common, but chins are the source of lots of other myths. For example, people expect a man with a jutting jaw to be aggressive. It's often said that you should never trust a man with a beard — presumably because for some sinister reason he's hiding his chin.

"Never trust someone whose eyes are too close together"

Such people are often described as having "shifty" eyes. Other myths associated with eyes are that if the eyes slope upward the person will be an opportunist; if you can see the whites of someone's eyes above their iris, they have a terrible temper; and if the eyes slope downward, that person will be eager to please everyone.

"People with low brows lack intelligence/are more likely to be criminals'"

A low brow — especially when combined with a short forehead, low hairline, and eyebrows that meet in the middle — is often said to show someone is unintelligent, aggressive, quick-tempered, and jealous.

★ And the truth is...

There's no evidence that the way people look has ANY link to how they behave. What happens is that we've already heard, for example, that someone with a jutting jaw will be aggressive. So when we meet someone with a jutting jaw, we pay special attention to behavior that fits our idea of them.

Verdict: PHONY

A scuba diver was once mistakenly dumped onto a forest fire

You know those planes that scoop up a bellyful of water from a lake, then fly over a forest fire and off-load it? Well, this myth tells of a scuba diver who was out diving not far below the surface, when he heard a strange, loud rumbling.

The story goes that a split second later, the diver was whisked out of the lake, along with the water he'd been swimming in, and into the belly of a fire-fighting plane. The plane flew on for a few minutes, then spilled out the water, scuba diver and all, onto a forest fire!

★ And the truth is...

There are versions of this story from the western US, Australia, Greece... just about anywhere that has forest fires. The only problem with it is, it's not true. Planes do scoop up water for fire fighting, but there's no evidence one of them has ever scooped up a diver as well. Phew!

Verdict: PHONY

Eskimos kiss by rubbing noses

The full version of this myth is that the Inuit live in such a cold place that they dare not kiss each other on the lips. If they did, their lips might freeze together — making it less a kiss than a marathon smooch, at least until they could get somewhere warm enough to get unglued. So instead, they rub noses in a greeting they call the "Eskimo kiss."

 And the truth is...
The Inuit do greet their closest friends and family using their noses. They place their upper lip and nose against the other person's skin and breathe in. But this is not a kiss, and has nothing to do with the danger of lips getting frozen together. It's just a different form of greeting.

Verdict:

IT'LL NEVER HAPPEN!

"There is no reason anyone would want a computer in their home."

Ken Olson, whose company made computers used by big businesses, in 1977.

You can unlock a car using a mobile phone

This is one of many myths about things you can do with a mobile phone, from cooking eggs (see page 13) to blowing up gas stations (see page 55).

It goes like this: If you lose your car keys while you're out, don't panic. All you need to do is call home, then ask someone there to get the key. Have them point the "blipper" at the phone, and point *your* phone at the car. The signal will be transmitted between the phones and to the car, which will unlock.

★ And the truth is...

There are a couple of problems with this myth. First of all, it doesn't work. Mobile phones transmit sound that humans can hear, but a car's automatic locking system uses a radio frequency we can't hear. Because they use different frequencies, the phone *can't* unlock the car.

The other problem is that even if you could unlock the car, you wouldn't be able to drive it — you still don't have the key. What you *would* have is an unlocked car, which you're about to abandon while you fetch the key.

Verdict:

> # A penguin was once stolen from a zoo!

This urban myth was very popular a few years ago. The story went that a 12-year-old boy became fascinated by the penguins at Boston Zoo. (Lots of urban myths have specific locations like this — it makes them more believable.)

In fact, the boy became so fascinated that he decided to take a penguin away with him. He popped one in his backpack, and went home.

The theft was only discovered when his mother went to investigate strange noises in the bathroom, and discovered her son sitting at one end of the bath… and a penguin at the other.

★ And the truth is…

It's a great story, but Boston Zoo counted all their penguins when this tall tale first appeared: none were missing. They also pointed out that versions of this story set in other zoos have appeared before.

Verdict:  **PHONY**

You can drink your own pee to survive

Imagine the scene: you're out for a hike in the remote mountains. Disaster strikes! You slip and fall, breaking your leg. The hot sun beats down, so you take a drink from your water bottle. Help will come soon.

The next day, still no one has come. Your throat is dry and sore, your water is all gone. You remember hearing somewhere that it's possible to drink your own pee to survive. Revolting — but can it be true?

★ The answer is...

This is 100% true — and if it's a choice between drinking your own pee and dying, the pee might not seem so revolting after all. Pee is about 95% water, and the rest of it is made up of things that would not normally do you any harm.

Some people even claim drinking pee is good for you. They put it in the fridge overnight, then drink it instead of orange juice at breakfast. Erm, bottoms up!

Verdict:  FACT

⭐ Sports inventions you probably haven't heard of before

Ever heard the phrase: "The answer to a question no one was asking"? The lack of success for these wacky sports inventions suggests they might fit that description:

1. Wings for skiers A crazy contraption to be used instead of ski poles; the wings were attached to a harness worn by the skier. He or she could use them to "create lift."

The jet-powered surfboard More than one attempt has been made to build a jet-powered or motorized surfboard. Ideal for surfers who for some reason are unable to paddle — perhaps because they're too busy strumming their ukuleles?

WOOAAAA

You should jump up to avoid impact in a falling elevator

First off, for all you nervous types, or elevataphobics (not a real name), please be assured that incidents in which elevators plunge downward are very rare. You're probably more likely to die of boredom in an elevator that's stuck. But if you are unfortunate enough to be in a elevator that's plummeting downward, a long-standing story says you can survive the impact unhurt. All you need to do is jump up in the air the moment before the elevator hits the bottom of its shaft. Easy peasy!

★ But the truth is...

Don't try it! The chances of remaining standing, let alone timing the jump properly, are virtually zero. Even if you did manage it, you almost certainly couldn't jump high enough to avoid the impact.

The best way to survive in an out-of-control elevator is to lie flat on your face, in the center of the floor. Cover the back of your head with your arms, to protect it. And good luck!

Verdict: **PHONY**

Eating fish makes you brainy

"Eat up your fish, it'll make you brainy."

This is a popular saying among grandmothers who are determined to make you eat boiled mackerel, pickled herring, battered dogfish, or some other delicious fishy dinner.

★ And the truth is...

Granny knows best. Oily fish such as mackerel, tuna, salmon, sardines, and herring all contains lots of fatty acids. Research in the US, UK, and elsewhere has shown that these can improve your concentration and memory. Just three months of increased consumption of fatty acids leads to improvements in school results. So, if you have exams coming up in three months or longer, get down to the fishmonger's and place your order!

 Verdict:

The formula for Coke is a closely guarded secret and no one knows the whole recipe

Coca-Cola is one of the most popular and successful soft drinks in the world and of course the company doesn't want other soft drink manufacturers to discover how to make the same drink.

One story says that the secret is so carefully guarded that only two people at Coke are allowed to know the formula. Not only that, but each of them only knows part of the formula. So in fact, no one has the entire recipe for how to make Coke.

 ## And the truth is...

This doesn't really make sense. What would happen if, for example, one of the two Coke employees were killed in a plane crash? His or her part of the formula would be lost. How does it work when one of the employees leaves the company, or retires? If they then tell the formula to someone else, that makes at least three or four people who know it.

Verdict:  **PHONY**

IT'LL NEVER HAPPEN!

"This 'telephone' has too many shortcomings to be seriously considered as a means of communication. The device is of no value to us."

Stated in a report in 1876 by Western Union, the telegraph company, on whether they should try to get into the telephone business.

By 1877 Western Union had changed their minds and decided to set up the American Speaking Telephone company. This would become part of the American Bell company, which by 1900 would have almost a million phones in service!

Mobile phones can blow up gas stations

Ever since mobile phones first appeared, stories have said that you mustn't use them in a gas station. The act of turning a phone on, or taking a call, can cause the phone's battery to spark. This spark could set fire to the gas fumes, causing a massive action-movie-style inferno.

★ And the truth is...

Mobile phones do use batteries, that bit's true. But then again, so do cars — and it's obviously safe to turn on your car in a gas station, or the whole filling-up-with-gas system would break down. And in fact, when have you ever seen a spark coming out of a mobile phone?

Because people have claimed there's a theoretical possibility of mobile phones triggering a fire, many gas stations have signs forbidding mobile phone use. But we haven't found any confirmed examples of a mobile phone actually causing a fire.

Whatever the truth is, though, this urban myth is so widespread that it's a good idea to put your phone away whenever you're near a gas station. Otherwise people might start staring at you, telling you not to be so irresponsible!

Verdict: almost certainly **PHONY** but put your phone away anyway

LOST IN SPACE!

"Him" up there!

There's some strange old stuff floating around in outer space, but nothing stranger than the creator of the TV series *Star Trek*, Gene Roddenberry, who died in 1991. Six years after his death some of his ashes were fired up into space on board a rocket!

Someone's hoping to rack up a lot of air miles, because there's a plan for more of Roddenberry's ashes — along with those of his wife — to be fired into deep space in the next few years.

IT'LL NEVER HAPPEN!

"Space travel is bunk."

Sir Harold Spencer Jones, UK's Astronomer Royal, in 1957. Two weeks later, the Russian Satellite Sputnik orbited the Earth.

Don't use the toilet when the train is in the station!

This urban myth is very well known. In fact, if you ever see anyone emerging from a train toilet at the station, they will almost certainly look embarrassed at having been caught using it. But why?

The answer is that when you flush a train toilet, all the waste is just dumped onto the track. People waiting at the platform will then find themselves sniffing the smell of pee — or worse.

★ And the truth is...

How true this is depends on the type of train carriage. Old-fashioned trains will just have a hatch in the floor, which opens when the toilet is flushed. Some designs mix the waste with sterilizing fluids. The most modern trains hold toilet waste on board until they reach the end of the line, when it is pumped out.

Verdict: better safe than sorry

WHERE IN THE WORLD?

You only get these little fortune-telling crackers in Chinese restaurants — so they must be from China, right?

UNCLE SAM'S
ALL-AMERICAN
CHINESE DINER

Free fortune cookie with every meal!

Wrong. Several people have claimed to be the inventor of the fortune cookie, but none of them lived in China. They were all from the USA. In a mock trial held in San Francisco, it was decided that the inventor of the fortune cookie was actually a Japanese American.

59

Health-related inventions you've probably never heard of before

Over the years there have been lots of crazy health-related inventions that seemed — mistakenly — like a good idea at the time. Here are our top picks:

Eyeball massager

Looking like a crazy pair of binoculars, this device puffed cool air on to your eyeballs, which presumably was a relaxing treatment for tired eyes.

Finger stretcher

Aimed at pianists who hoped to give their fingers a wider range on the keyboard, this was presumably also bought by amateur torturers.

Spectacles with lights

See in the dark with these amazing spectacles that have tiny lights on top! Just don't go out in the rain, unless you want an electric shock.

You should never wake a sleepwalker

Lots of people will tell you that you should never wake a sleepwalker. You'll hear various reasons for this:

① The sleepwalker will have a heart attack
The shock of being woken up in a strange place will be so great that the sleeping person's heart will stop.

② They will have a seizure
The brain, suddenly wrenched from sleep, will go haywire, causing the sleepwalker to have a seizure.

③ They will attack you
Surprised and confused, woken sleepwalkers can sometimes lash out and attack the person who has woken them up.

★ And the truth is...
It's actually quite difficult to wake a sleepwalker, but there's no health reason not to do it. The person may be surprised and disoriented, though, so it's best to try to gently lead them back to bed without waking them.

Verdict:

St. Bernard dogs carry tiny barrels of brandy

St. Bernard dogs were originally bred by monks living at the top of the St. Bernard Pass in Switzerland. Pilgrims crossing between Italy and Switzerland constantly used this ancient route through the mountains. They took shelter at the monastery, especially during the winter.

The St. Bernard Pass is one of the highest in the Alps, and in winter is regularly blocked by snowfall. Travelers would sometimes be caught outside, and the monks would have to send out rescue parties. St. Bernard dogs were bred to help with these rescues: the dogs' thick coats, strength, and keen sense of smell made them great at rescuing lost pilgrims. Each dog wore a small barrel of brandy around its neck, which travelers could use to revive themselves.

★ And the truth is...

All true — apart from the bit about the brandy. A British artist called Edwin Landseer included the detail in a painting in 1820. People liked the idea of brandy-carrying dogs so much that it stuck — even though alcohol is actually bad for people with hypothermia.

Verdict:  PHONY

WHERE IN THE WORLD?

No.5: Swiss roll

No one knows why this is called Swiss roll, but it's definitely not because it comes from Switzerland. No one there has heard of it.

In fact, it's only the British who even called it Swiss roll — though they then spread the name to other parts of the world.

INSECTS CAN
YOUR EAR AND

The most common version of this story is that ants can crawl into your ear and eat your brain. But other insects, and even snails, have been reported as brain eaters, too.

In one incident, a boy is said to have fallen asleep with some sweets nearby. Ants were soon attracted by the sweets, and his mother found hundreds of them near the boy's head when she woke him.

Soon after, the boy began to complain that his face felt itchy all the time. His mother finally took him to the doctor, who couldn't work out what the problem was. Finally the doctor took an X-ray — only to discover to his horror that there were live ants inside the boy's skull!

CRAWL INSIDE
EAT YOUR BRAIN!

ARGGGHHH

read on!

A variation of this myth is...

Snails eat your brain

In this version of the myth, a man has balance problems and keeps getting terrible headaches. He goes to the doctor, and finally it's decided he needs an operation. When they open up his skull, the doctors find that a snail has gotten inside and eaten part of his brain.

★ And the truth is...

Relax. It's very, very rare that insects *do* get into human ears. They quickly realize that it's not somewhere they want to be, and try to get out. The buzzing and movement can be painful and upsetting for both human and insect. However, it's simply not possible for insects to burrow into people's heads. (Think about it; even if they did, how would they survive in there for long enough to eat your brain?)

Snails also *cannot* burrow into people's heads through ear holes. Some snails, though, do carry a tiny worm which can be transmitted to humans if they eat raw or undercooked snails. Once inside the body, the worm is carried in the blood to the brain, where it causes a deadly brain disease called meningitis.

Verdict: almost entirely PHONY

Walt Disney's body was frozen when he died

When the famous cartoon animator and studio head Walt Disney died from cancer on December 15, 1966, at the age of 65, his death came as a shock to his closest friends and family.

Within a few weeks of Disney's death, it was announced that the first-ever cryogenic freezing of a body had taken place. Cryogenic freezing preserves the body as it was at death, the idea being that this preserves the body which can be brought "back to life" at some point in the future.

Soon, rumors began to circulate that Disney had also been cryogenically frozen, in the hope that a cure for his cancer would be discovered and he could be revived. Some versions of the story say that his frozen body is kept below one of the rides at the Disneyland amusement park.

★ And the truth is...
Walt Disney was cremated on December 17, 1966. His ashes were then stored at Forest Lawn Memorial Park in California.

Verdict: PHONY

Yawning is infectious

Have you ever noticed that as soon as one person in a group yawns, others start to do the same thing? People will tell you that it's because yawning is infectious. But why would you "catch" a yawn from someone, when you're not even tired?

★ The truth is...

Many scientific studies have shown that yawning is indeed infectious. It's also something people do without thinking. They see someone else yawning, and their body just joins in. Scientists have only recently begun to understand why. The answer lies in our prehistoric past.

Yawning gets extra oxygen into the bloodstream. The oxygen helps the muscles and brain get energy, making us better able to move and think quickly. That's why you yawn when tired, to perk yourself up. Our ancient ancestors would have needed a boost like this when under threat — if a dangerous animal was around, for example. If one person yawned to get ready for action, the other members of the band would subconsciously know that they needed to be ready too, and would yawn — and that's why we do the same.

Verdict: ⸻ FACT ⸻

IT'LL NEVER HAPPEN!

"who...wants to hear actors talk?"

In 1927 H.M. Warner, co-founder of Warner Brothers movie studio, fails to see that the people who want to see actors walk will also want to hear them talk.

"Television won't last because people will soon get tired of staring at a plywood box every night."

In 1946 Darryl Zanuck, legendary movie producer, fails to foresee that the popularity of TV will one day be prolonged when they are made of plastic, rather than plywood!

"Television won't last. It's a flash in the pan."

Mary Somerville, pioneer of radio educational broadcasts, 1948.

It's possible for a man to become pregnant

Just a few years ago, the world was amazed to hear that a person named Lee Mingwei had become the first man to get pregnant.

The story said that after having hormone treatment, Mr. Lee had a human embryo implanted in his belly. There, it would grow into a baby before being removed by Caesarian section.

Incredibly, a website gave details, including photos of the pregnant Mr. Lee. You could even see ultrasound images of the baby inside him. So it must be true, right?

★ And the truth is...

The misguided genius behind the project was an artist named Virgil Wong. He and his friend Lee Mingwei put the whole story together themselves. They claimed that it was art — maybe the question here should really be, are they right?

Verdict: **PHONY**

copper pennies cure insect bites

"Miracle" cures such as this are among some of the most popular myths whizzing around the world. This one says that taping a copper penny over a bee or wasp sting will stop it from itching.

This is just one of the amazing cures copper is said to perform. Others include curing rheumatism (pain in the joints and muscles) by wearing a copper bracelet, and removing warts by rubbing them 20 times with a copper coin.

★ And the truth is...

Unfortunately, there's no scientific evidence that copper can perform these feats. Of course, people will still tell you it definitely is true, because they tried it and it worked. If they do, point out that these days most "copper" coins are made almost entirely of zinc (in the US) or steel (in Europe).

Verdict:  PHONY

Chips were invented by accident

Chips are one of the world's favorite snacks. Something so delicious must surely have been the result of chefs spending long hours trying to make tasty snacks from potatoes?

Not if the rumors are true. A popular urban myth says that chips were actually invented by accident, in 1853, by an angry chef named George Crum. A customer had sent back his fries, complaining they were too thick and soggy. The chef decided to retaliate by slicing some potatoes as thin as possible and frying them. To his surprise the picky customer was delighted — and the popularity of the potato chip had begun.

★ The truth is...

Crum was not the first person to make chips. There were similar recipes in several cookbooks years before his 1853 "discovery."

Verdict:  PHONY

An office worker died at his desk and no one noticed for days

George Turklebaum, this urban myth says, was a worker at a New York publishing company. George kept to himself, but was a dedicated worker. He was usually first to the office in the morning, and last to leave at night. He would often spend hours hunched over his desk, checking through papers.

Perhaps it's not surprising that George's fellow workers didn't immediately notice that he hadn't moved much at his desk one day. What is surprising, though, is that it took them five days to notice that he was still in the exact same position. George wasn't just concentrating really hard. He was dead.

And the truth is...

Except in very cold conditions, bodies start to decompose in a lot less than five days. In fact, within three days George would have started to stink and unpleasant fluids would have started to leak from his body.

On top of that, at the time this story appeared, there was no George Turklebaum listed in the New York phone book.

Verdict:  **PHONY**

THE MOON LANDINGS WERE FAKED

Oh boy. There are so many urban myths, legends, and conspiracy theories about the Moon landings that you could fill an entire book with them. In fact, some people have, in an attempt to show that the landings themselves never took place.

For those of you with more interesting things to spend your time on than an entire book of Moon landing myths, here's our summary of the main ones:

1. The American flag

The American flag is seen waving in the breeze — but there's no wind on the Moon, which does not have an atmosphere.

In fact, the flag only waves around as an astronaut is screwing it into the Moon's surface. The rest of the time it's still.

2. No stars

Even though the sky is dark, you cannot see any stars in photos of the Moon landings.

This is because all landings took place during lunar daytime, with the surface lit up by the Sun's rays (which is why it was possible to take photos in the first place). Stars shine too dimly during lunar daytime to be picked up on film.

3. Invisible photographers

When astronaut Neil Armstrong first stepped onto the Moon, he was filmed. But his fellow astronaut Buzz Aldrin was inside the lunar lander. So who was doing the filming?

The footage of Armstrong stepping down onto the surface was shot by an automatic device. It had already been maneuvered into position.

In some photos of astronaut Buzz Aldrin, you can see from the reflection in his visor that Neil Armstrong isn't holding a camera. So who took that photo?

The astronauts had cameras mounted on their chests, so that they didn't have to hold them in their hands.

4. Rockets without flames

When the lunar module took off, no flames appeared to come from its exhaust.

This is because the fuel that was used produces a flame that is transparent, hard to see, and almost impossible to photograph.

Verdict: **PHONY** on all counts

LOST IN SPACE!

Astronaut pee!

Ever wonder what happens to an astronaut's pee? In the old days, it used to just be ejected out into space. It immediately froze into tiny crystals, which astronauts described as one of the most beautiful sights they'd seen.

Nowadays, astronauts are much more careful with their pee. Instead of being released into space, it's put into a recycling unit. This turns their pee into... drinking water. Yeuw.

WEEEEE

The Coca-Cola company invented the modern Santa Claus

Everybody loves Santa Claus. When that jolly, plump man with the white beard and the red-and-white outfit starts appearing on billboards and in TV ads, we know Christmas is on its way.

There's a well-known urban myth that says most people don't realize there's a secret message hidden in the images of the

modern Santa, and that message is: "Buy more Coke." How can this be so? Well, it's because the modern Santa Claus — the white-bearded man in a red outfit — was created by Coca-Cola. You can tell because they painted him in their own colors, red and white, as an advertising logo!

★ And the truth is...

Coke did not invent the modern Santa. In fact, he first appeared in a Coke ad in 1931, and red-and-white Santas had been around for at least 30 years by then.

Verdict: **PHONY**

WHERE IN THE WORLD?

OK, for a drink to be called "champagne" it has to come from the Champagne region of France. But the French like to think that they invented this method of making fizzy wine. Specifically, Dom Perignon is said to have developed sparkling wine in the late 1600s.

Shame, then, that Britain's Royal Society heard exactly how to make fizzy wine thirty years earlier, in a paper by a scientist called Christopher Merrit.

Lightning never strikes in the same place twice

The basic idea behind this saying is that the odds on any one place being struck by lightning are tiny. If you then try to work out the chances of the same place being struck a second time by a bolt of lightning, it quickly becomes clear that it's so unlikely as to be impossible.

★ And the truth is...

Lightning usually strikes a high point, such as a church steeple, a tall building or a lone tree. If it has been drawn to a particular high point during a storm once, it is very likely to be drawn to that same high point again. The Empire State Building in New York City, for example, is regularly hit by lightning more than 100 times per year.

Verdict:

The Halloween poisoner is based on fact

This is one of the most popular and feared urban legends of all, especially among kids (and their parents).

The idea is that a crazy person, tired of kids banging on the door and demanding treats, decides to play an evil trick on them. The sweets that are handed out are laced with poison. Within hours some of the kids who have eaten them start dying.

★ And the truth is...

Poisonings have happened at Halloween. Most have been accidental, but a very small number have been deliberate. However, they have not been the work of a random loony. The best-known case happened in 1974, when a father killed his son using cyanide in a Halloween treat. In prison the father later became known as The Candyman.

Verdict: _____ partly  FACT

strawberry milkshakes contain crushed beetles

Next time you order a strawberry milkshake, should you worry that you'll actually be drinking down little particles of crushed-up beetle? That's what this urban myth says — but surely modern food safety laws mean this can't possibly be the case?

And the truth is...

It's not just strawberry milkshakes! Lots of the red-colored things you drink or eat may contain crushed beetle.

Hundreds of years ago, people in Central and South America worked out that the ground-up remains of a certain kind of beetle, which lived in a particular type of cactus, could be used to dye things red. The dye is now called cochineal, and it is still used in lots of red food and drinks.

Verdict: FACT

Eating carrots helps you to see in the dark

Generations of children know this urban myth well!

No one knows how many carrots have died a horrible death, being slowly boiled in steaming water, so that children won't need glasses. It must be millions. But did those innocent little carrots die needlessly?

★ The truth is...

Flight Lieutenant John Cunningham — sometimes called "Cat's Eyes Cunningham" — knew the answer to this one. He became famous in Britain during World War II (1939-45) for his amazing ability to spot German bombers at night. It was said that this was partly due to Cunningham's love of carrots. People were so impressed with the idea that they started eating extra carrots, hoping it would help them find their way around during the nighttime blackout.

Unfortunately, the whole thing was made up. The British were actually spotting German bombers using a new kind of radar, which they didn't want the enemy to find out about. The carrot story was just a distraction. A pure fabrication!

Verdict: PHONY

LOST IN SPACE!

Golf balls

More than one space traveler has been gripped by golf fever. As early as 1971, US astronaut Al Shepard was hitting a golf ball about 1,000 feet (300 m) across the surface of the Moon.

The record for distance goes to cosmonaut Mikhail Tyurin, though. In 2006, Tyurin was on a spacewalk outside the International Space Station. He gave a golf ball a good whack with the club, and off it sailed. Scientists later estimated it would travel roughly a million miles, before burning up in Earth's atmosphere.

ELVIS IS ALIVE!

Elvis Presley was the best-selling music star of all time. He had ten US number one albums, and many more in other countries. His singles topped the charts 18 times in the US and 21 times in the UK. US President Jimmy Carter once said that Elvis had:

"Changed the face of American... culture."

When Elvis died in 1977, roughly 80,000 people lined the streets between his home at Graceland and the Forest Hill Cemetery in Tennessee. They couldn't believe he had died at just 42 years of age.

Thang you very much...Ahuh!

But... did Elvis really die on August 16, 1977? There are plenty of people who think not.

Some Elvis fans think that The King, as he was known, did not die at all. Instead, sick of his current existence, the theory goes that he went into hiding and created a new life for himself. Various claims have been made (not all of them 100% serious):

★ **Elvis regularly makes prank phone calls. His favorite is apparently to ask people, "Is your refrigerator running?" When they say yes, he asks, "How, without any legs?"**

★ **Elvis is regularly seen shopping at K-Mart stores.**

★ **Elvis is sometimes claimed to have retrained as a doctor, and spent his time delivering babies.**

 ## The truth is...

Elvis would be in his late 70s if he were alive today, so — unlike Hitler — it wouldn't be impossible for him to still be around. BUT, there's no real doubt that he did die in 1977. Elvis was known to have serious health problems, and his family, doctors, friends, and managers all saw the body, which was also secretly photographed.

Verdict: **PHONY**

A boy once peed flies!

In 2003, newspapers and the internet started to carry a story about a 13-year-old boy named Chandan Goswami, who had an unusual and very worrying problem. Apparently, when he went to pee, living flies started coming out.

For the next ten days, the *Calcutta Telegraph* kept its readers informed of the boy's condition. It reported that doctors had discovered that the "flies" were actually winged beetles and they were breeding in the boy's abdomen. The beetles continued to emerge until, sick of the attention and the lack of a cure, the boy's parents moved him to another hospital. And at that point, his story disappeared from public view.

★ And the truth is...

There is a medical condition called myiasis, in which maggots such as fly larvae infest living flesh. It rarely affects humans, but is not unknown. The known facts about Chandan Goswami suggest he may have been affected by myiasis.

Verdict: probably FACT

IT'LL NEVER HAPPEN!

"Rail travel at high speed is not possible, because passengers, unable to breathe, would die of asphyxia."

Dr. Dionysus Larder, Professor of Natural Philosophy and Astronomy at University College, London.

A man once flew 3 miles (4.8 km) upward in a garden chair

Many people dream of having their own personal flying device. Few of us ever decide to make one out of a garden chair and some balloons — and then take it on a 3-mile-high (4.8 km) test flight. But that's just what happened one day in Los Angeles.

Larry Walters bought himself 45 weather balloons and a bottle of helium gas. He tied the balloons tightly to a garden chair, and tied the chair to his pickup truck. Next Larry filled the balloons with helium, which caused the chair to lift off. Larry climbed aboard and strapped himself to the chair. He took along an air pistol, to shoot some of the balloons when he was ready to descend.

Larry released the rope from the pickup, and took off.

After floating around at the same height as international jet flights (he was spotted by at least one surprised pilot), Larry began to get cold. So he shot out some of his balloons... and floated back down to Earth. Phew-ey.

★ And the truth is...

This all really happened, on July 2, 1982.

Verdict: incredible, but it's ...

88

Cheese gives you nightmares

In the Charles Dickens story *A Christmas Carol*, the miser Scrooge is visited in the night by disturbing visions. He blames the visions on bad dreams, caused by eating "a crumb of cheese" just before going to bed.

Scrooge is not alone. Many people think that eating cheese too close to bedtime will give them nightmares. But is this long-standing urban myth actually true?

⭐ The fact is...

An investigation in 2005 discovered that there is a connection between cheese and dreams. People were given a small piece of cheese to eat before bed, then asked to record their dreams. Three-quarters of them said they slept well, and most remembered their dreams more clearly than usual. People who ate blue cheese had especially vivid dreams.

No one, though, reported that their dreams were nightmares.

Verdict:  PHONY

A FEW SURPRISING SLEEP FACTS

 Top-notch scientist Einstein liked to give his brain plenty of rest. He used to sleep for 12 hours every day.

 Former British prime minister Margaret Thatcher was famous for needing only 4 hours of sleep each night — though she also used to take a nap during the day. Another prime minister, Winston Churchill, got into bed for a nap every afternoon.

 Elizabethans who couldn't sleep used to rub dormouse fat on the soles of their feet (Take note, this wouldn't work).

 Counting imaginary sheep is a terrible way of trying to get to sleep (though possibly not as terrible as rubbing dormouse fat on your feet). Imagining a relaxing scene is a much better technique.

Chocolate chip cookies were invented by accident

One day in 1930, innkeeper Ruth Wakefield was baking chocolate cookies for her guests at the Toll House Inn in Massachusetts. Halfway through, she realized there was no cooking chocolate left. She did have some ordinary chocolate, so Ruth broke it up into little chunks and put those in.

Instead of melting as the cookies baked, like normal, the chips of chocolate stayed almost whole. The chocolate chip cookie had been invented — by accident.

CHOCOLATE
Lifetime Supply

⭐ The truth is...

This is a true story. Not only that, but Ruth Wakefield gave her recipe to the Nestle chocolate company in return for a lifetime supply of chocolate chips.

Verdict: —— FACT ——

Eating celery actually makes you thinner

The full version of this myth says that celery contains so few calories that you actually use up more energy eating it than you get.

The theory goes that the human body uses roughly 10% of its energy on digestion and storing of nutrients. But celery is 95% water. The rest contains so few calories, that it can't even provide enough energy to fuel the digestive process. Instead, energy from other foods is needed. So eating celery uses more calories than it produces.

The truth is...

The amount of energy you spend on eating celery is tiny, and will not help you lose weight. In addition, if you ate only celery you'd quickly become malnourished. Your hair would get thin and limp, your skin would look pasty, and you wouldn't have any get-up-and-go.

Verdict:  PHONY

You can see the Great Wall of China from space

For years, people have believed that it's possible to see the Great Wall of China from space, using only the naked eye. The myth actually appears in schoolbooks and board games around the world. In fact, some people will even tell you that the Great Wall is the only artificial structure that can be seen from space. But is it true?

 The fact is...

In 2003, Yang Liwei became the first Chinese person to visit space, in the spacecraft Shenzhou V. He looked pretty hard for the Great Wall — but when he returned to Earth, Yang had to admit that he hadn't been able to see it, even though he'd flown above it. The Chinese government immediately began to remove the claim from school textbooks.

Verdict:  **PHONY**

GLOSSARY

asphyxia a lack of oxygen or excess of carbon dioxide in the body that results in unconsciousness and often death and is usually caused by interruption of breathing or inadequate oxygen supply

bunk not true; nonsense

bunker a protective embankment or dugout mostly below ground

conspiracy theory a theory that explains an event or set of circumstances as the result of a secret plot by usually powerful conspirators

decompose to break up into constituent parts by or as if by a chemical process

diaphragm a thin, curved muscle below the lungs

dissolve to mix completely into a liquid

exhaust the gases that escape from the fuel burned in an engine

fabrication the act of making up for the purpose of deception

germinate to cause to sprout or develop

hypothermia dangerously low body temperature caused by cold conditions

lunar of, relating to, or resembling the moon

malnourished supplied with less than the minimum amount of the foods essential for health and growth

mock of, relating to, or having the character of an imitation

myiasis infestation with fly maggots

novelty something new or unusual

numerology the study of supernatural significance of numbers

plummet to drop sharply and abruptly

receptacle a container

seizure a sudden attack resulting from abnormal electrical discharges in the brain

spectacles glasses

sterilize to free from living microorganisms like bacteria

superstition a belief or practice resulting from ignorance, fear of the unknown, trust in magic or chance, or a false conception of causation

transmit to send or convey from one person or place to another

ukulele a small guitar of Portuguese origin popularized in Hawaii in the 1880s and strung typically with four strings

FOR MORE INFORMATION

BOOKS

Brunvand, Jan Harold. *Too Good to Be True: The Colossal Book of Urban Legends.* New York: W. W. Norton & Company, 2011.

Jennings, Ken. *Because I Said So!: The Truth Behind the Myths, Tales, and Warnings Every Generation Passes Down to Its Kids.* New York: Simon and Schuster, 2012.

O'Shei, Tim. *Creepy Urban Legends.* Mankato, MN: Capstone Press, 2011.

WEBSITES

Urban Legends Online
http://urbanlegendsonline.com/

Scary Urban Legends for Kids
http://www.scaryforkids.com/urban-legends/

Top 5 Halloween Urban Legends
http://www.scaryforkids.com/urban-legends/

Publisher's note to educators and parents: Our editors have carefully reviewed these websites to ensure that they are suitable for students. Many websites change frequently, however, and we cannot guarantee that a site's future contents will continue to meet our high standards of quality and educational value. Be advised that students should be closely supervised whenever they access the Internet.

Where can I find myths about...